mega geex

101 Mazes of the World's Greatest

Copyright © 2021 by Megageex ltd

First paperback edition, 2021.

Megageex.com

ISBN: 978-965-92913-3-5

Table of Contents

Fair use of this product

At MegaGeex, we love making content designed to help build better learners. Our resources empower parents and educators alike to give kids hands-on inspiration to grow into the world-changing adults we want them to be. To be able to do that, we need your help to guarantee that we have the resources to continue to create great content.

If our resources are used beyond home and personal use, in a classroom, or other educational settings where you receive compensation, then a professional license is required.

Each professional license allows for a single teacher to use the resource for students in the teacher's class or block of classes. Price is determined by the number of students using the resource. If more than one teacher in your school wants access to the materials, then additional licenses are available for purchase.

Questions? Feel free to reach out to us at hello@megageex.com and we'll be happy to help. If someone you know would like to use one of our printable pages, have them check out www.megageex.com for our full catalog.

If we could look back over 600 years, most would be amazed at the developments, discoveries, and inventions that have changed the world. Human-kind, in this small space of time, has made advancements in every area of our lives. Communication is possible with people thousands of miles away- in real time! Circling the planet is accomplished in only days. Television, movies, computers, automobiles, only begin to tell the story of the mind-blowing improvements that benefit us all.

These awesome accomplishments were made possible by regular people who had extraordinary qualities. Men and women who shared two common traits: Passion and Grit. In the face of challenges and even failures, they never quit, and they succeeded in what many viewed as impossible.

With dedication and persistence, they overcame whatever hurdles given to them by society during their lives. Women such as Ada Lovelace, Marie Curie, and Jane Austen pursued their education despite laws and views that said they could not. George Washington Carver never gave up in the face of racial discrimination. And Albert Einstein could not find a job as a professor but he still continued work on his theories. These are just a few examples of the character of these remarkable individuals.

In 2018, Daniel Scalosub, embarked on a mission of his own. He wanted his twin daughters to know that they can do ANYTHING. And what better way to prove this to them than to share the incredible stories of these inventors, writers, scientists and artists, and entrepreneurs. Daniel founded Megageex to bring knowledge, and more importantly, inspiration and encouragement to kids everywhere.

Feel free to explore our unique products. Each one is designed with the sole purpose to inspire and teach through play and creativity.

Connect your kids with the world's greatest minds and get ready for a learning journey like no other.

Welcome to Megageex!

Grownups! Before starting, read here!

Albert Einstein

Dear grownups,
Before your little ones dive into this book, here are some tips...

Learn through play

Each maze was carefully crafted to provide a mental challenge along with a growth mindset learning experience from the MegaGeex life story. Kids get to solve fun mazes while learning about science, history, art, and more.

Key benefits

Jane Austen

- Improves problem-solving skills through the exercise of cognitive thought processes

- Improves eye-hand coordination and visual discrimination skills

- Boosts patience and persistence skills, and feelings of confidence and success when a maze is completed

- Growth mindset lessons based on the life's story of the world's greatest minds

- Screen-free activity

How to use this book?

 Level 1 contains our easiest mazes and are perfect for beginners! The paths are easy to "see", There are fewer details and fewer incorrect choices to make along the route.

 Level 2 becomes more challenging with paths that blend in with the illustration, have more twists, turns, and more chances to go the wrong way!

Level 3 contains our most difficult mazes! Look very carefully to find your way through each puzzle. Finding the right path will not be easy!

 Start and Finish--each maze clearly shows where to begin with a **Start** and the **Finish**.

  Pencils with erasers are recommended so that routes can be changed as needed when taking a wrong turn.

After solving the maze, the correct path and pictures can be colored.

Rosalind Franklin

Let's play!

Send us a picture of your child and their favorite page to hello@megageex.com and we'll highlight their achievement in the **MegaGeex community**.

Meet the MegaGeex

Isaac Newton

English mathematician and scientist (1642 - 1727). Formulated the laws of gravity, motion, and energy. Developed calculus, a new type of math for understanding and describing continuous change.

Madam CJ Walker

American businesswoman, entrepreneur, and social activist (1867 - 1919). Created the first cosmetics and hair care line of products for African-American women. First self-made American female millionaire.

Wolfgang Amadeus Mozart

Austrian composer and child prodigy (1756 - 1791). Considered one of the most popular composers in western history, having composed more than 600 works. His music had a tremendous influence on subsequent western music.

Jane Austen

English writer and author (1775 - 1817) who wrote such classic books as *Pride & Prejudice*, *Emma*, and *Sense & Sensibility* which challenged country life in 1800s century England.

Charles Darwin

English naturalist and biologist (1809 - 1882). Pioneered the science of evolution. His work *On the Origin of Species* shows how beings evolve over time through natural selection.

Nikola Tesla

Serbian scientist, inventor, and futurist (1856 - 1942). Designed the alternating current (AC) model that provides electricity to homes. Pioneered radio transmissions and wireless technology.

Rosalind Franklin

English chemist (1920 - 1958). Proved the double-helix model of DNA, the building blocks of all life. Her work on the structure of viruses contributed to founding the field of structural virology.

Thomas Edison

American inventor and entrepreneur (1847 - 1931). Considered "America's greatest inventor". Invented the light bulb, the phonograph, the first motion picture camera, early electric power generators, and over a thousand other inventions.

Galileo Galilei

Italian scientist (1564 - 1642). Considered the "father of modern physics". Pioneered the "scientific method" of learning through observation, asking questions and seeking answers by doing experiments.

The Wright Brothers

American aviation pioneers and inventors (Orville 1871 - 1948, Wilbur 1867 - 1912). They invented and built the first motorized airplane and were the first men to fly it in December 1903.

Meet the MegaGeex

Henry Ford

American inventor and industrialist (1863 - 1947). Started the Ford Motor Company and mass-produced the Model T car. Developed the assembly line, which revolutionized the factory production of goods in American industries. Influenced the Labor Movement when he started the five-day/40-hour workweek in his factories.

Michelangelo

Italian painter, sculptor, poet, and architect (1475 - 1564). Considered the greatest artist of his lifetime, his most famous works are the paintings on the ceiling of the Sistine Chapel, the sculpture of David, the reconstruction of St. Peter's Basilica and military fortifications for the city of Florence.

Rachel Carson

American conservationist and environmentalist (1907 - 1964). Inspired the environmental movement with her book *Silent Spring*. Warned of the dangers of pesticides. Credited with the eventual creation of the Environmental Protection Agency.

Mark Twain

Author, humorist, and entrepreneur (1835 - 1910). Born as Samuel Clemons. Considered "the father of American literature." His most famous novels were *The Adventures of Tom Sawyer* and *The Adventures of Huckleberry Finn*. Also created and marketed a trivia game, elastic belt, and scrapbook.

Ludwig van Beethoven

German composer (1770 - 1827). Began to lose his hearing at age 28 and was deaf by age 45. It was during this time that he created some of his greatest works. Considered to be one of the greatest musical geniuses of all time and his most influential works include the *Eroica Symphony and Symphony No. 9.*

Ada Lovelace

English mathematician and writer (1815 - 1852). Regarded as the "world's first computer programmer". Wrote the first computer algorithm based on Charles Babbage's Analytical Machine.

Leonardo da Vinci

Italian inventor, artist, and naturalist (1452 - 1519) whose wide-ranging works include the *Mona Lisa*, the first helicopter, and is considered one of the most brilliant people to have ever lived.

Alan Turing

English mathematician (1912 - 1954). Considered the "father of computer science" and pioneered artificial intelligence. Built early computers to break German codes and help win World War II.

Albert Einstein

German physicist (1879 - 1955). One of the world's most influential scientists, whose work on light, gravity, time and space changed the way we understand our universe. Formulated the *Theory of Relativity* and Nobel Prize winner in Physics.

Helen Keller

American author, political and disability rights activist (1880 - 1968). Lost her sight and her hearing after an illness when she was a young child. Learned to read and write using braille and authored twelve books. Was the first deaf/blind person to earn a college degree.

Marco Polo

Explorer and writer (1254 - 1324). Marco Polo traveled to Asia when he was 16 years old and documented all he saw. This information opened up trade and relations between Asia and Europe leading to a great exchange of goods and technology.

Alexander Graham Bell

Scottish scientist, inventor, and teacher of the deaf (1847 - 1922). Invented the first practical telephone and founded AT&T, the world's first telephone company.

Frida Kahlo

Mexican painter, and icon for the feminist movement of the 1970's (1907 - 1954). She was best known for her portraits and art inspired by artifacts in Mexico. By the 1970s her work was recognized by feminists for the depiction of women's experiences and how her art chronicled her life as it was affected by chronic pain.

George Washington Carver

American agricultural chemist and agronomist (1860s - 1942). Developed methods for improving soil fertility, and crops versatility. Created products with peanuts, which gave him the nickname "the Peanut Man".

Marie Curie

Polish physicist and chemist (1867 - 1934). The first woman to win the Nobel Prize for her discovery of radioactivity, and the first person to win the Nobel twice. Discovered the elements radium and polonium.

The Wright Brothers' father ignited their interest in flying with a small helicopter-type toy. The boys played with the toy helicopter over and over. The toy would break, and they would fix it and play again. The boys loved flying kites as well.

Solution on page 116

START

FINISH

Alexander Graham Bell

Alexander Graham Bell had a personal interest in the science of sound and communication because his mother and wife both had hearing loss. This passion led to the first patent filed for a working telephone. Bell could play the piano and was an excellent musician.

Solution on page 116

Wolfgang Amadeus Mozart was a musical genius, but he had other interests and hobbies. He liked to play billiards. And, he had a dog named Bimperl that he loved very much. He once wrote a letter and told the recipient to give Bimperl a thousand kisses.

Solution on page 116

Madam CJ Walker

Madam CJ Walker, whose name was Sarah Breedlove before she was married, worked as a laundress. Her hair began to fall out-possibly from the chemicals and steam used when washing clothes. She began to research ingredients to make a hair product that would re-grow hair. She developed a formula and started her business.

Solution on page 116

Nikola Tesla was born in what is now known as Croatia in 1856. He was brilliant and could solve complicated computations in his head. Once in school, his physics teacher showed him the Garmme Dynamo. This invention inspired him to invent the induction motor that changed the world.

Solution on page 116

START

FINISH

Rosalind Franklin

Rosalind Franklin is best known for her work on DNA. She was able to isolate and take the first photograph of a DNA strand. This photo is considered by many to be the most important picture ever taken. It is called Photo 51.

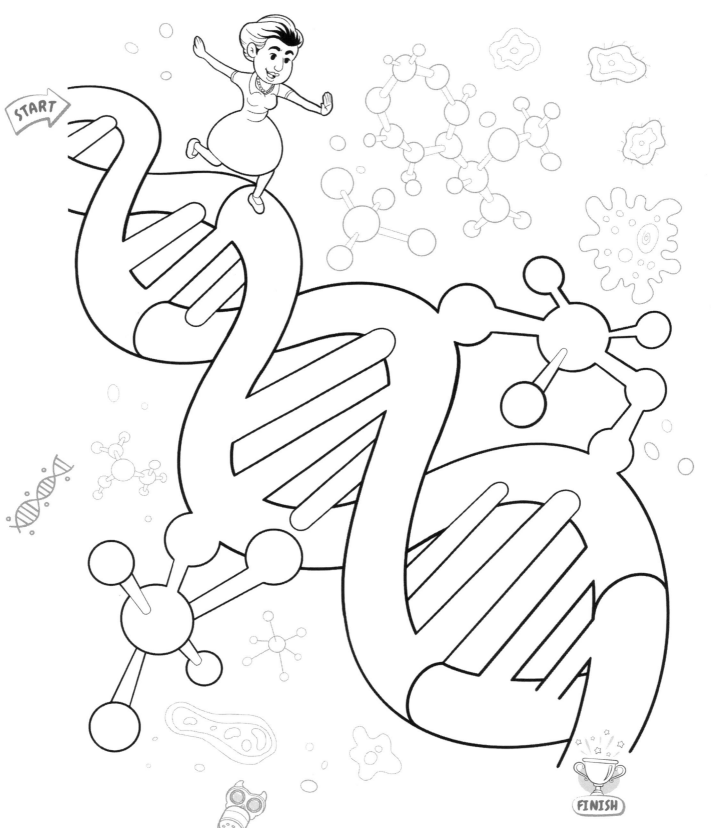

Solution on page 116

START

FINISH

Thomas Edison grew up in the state of Ohio, in the USA. Young Thomas did not do very well in school. His teacher thought he was not very smart. His mother disagreed. She began homeschooling him. She even helped him set up a lab in his basement. He loved to study and experiment.

Solution on page 116

START

FINISH

Marco Polo

Marco Polo is best known for his travels around the world. His documentation and geographical information was widely used in the 15th and 16th century by European explorers. He was born in Venice but at age 16 he traveled to China and traveled the Silk Road. This area of the world had never been traveled by any European. He stayed in China and went on expeditions by the order of the great Kublai Khan.

Solution on page 116

Born in 1475 in Florence Italy. His mother passed away early in his life and he lived with his nanny and her husband who was a stone cutter. At an early age, the young boy learned to use a chisel and hammer. As a kid, he didn't like to go to school, he preferred to copy paintings from churches. He often did not go to school but visited churches during the day instead.

START

FINISH

Charles Darwin

Darwin went to medical school but he did not like it. Looking at the inside of a body made him ill. He moved schools to Cambridge, and there he found his passion--studying zoology, botany, and geography.

Solution on page 116

Marie Curie was taught to read and write when she was very young. She was very bright and did well with school work. She had a very good memory and worked hard.

Solution on page 116

Ludwig van Beethoven

Beethoven showed talent at a very early age. His father was a serious and often harsh teacher for the young child. Beethoven first played the piano, organ, and violin. He performed his first concert at age 7. At age 13, he became friends with a family with children. He stayed with them often and taught the children how to play the piano.

Solution on page 116

Mark Twain, whose real name was Samuel Clemons, was an American author. His most famous works include *The Adventures of Tom Sawyer* and *Adventures of Huckleberry Finn*. Mark Twain wrote 28 books and over 100 short stories.

Solution on page 117

Marco Polo

Many countries were positively affected by Marco Polo. Marco Polo opened trade between Europe and China. With trade between Europe and China, the Europeans were introduced to citrus fruits, spices, and other newly seen goods. Silk, porcelain, ivory, horses, and jewels were traded.

Solution on page 117

Rachel Carson was a student of nature. She was a marine scientist. She became a published writer for children's magazines at age 10. She got a master's degree in zoology.

Solution on page 117

START

FINISH

Charles was born in Shrewsbury, England in 1809. He did not like school as his education focused on classical subjects such as Greek and Latin. He enjoyed doing chemistry experiments with his older brother, who built a lab in the garden tool shed.

START

FINISH

Solution on page 117

Orville and Wilbur Wright are best known for the first successful motorized aircraft flight. This flight occurred in Kitty Hawk, North Carolina. The first flight lasted only 12 seconds. That same day, the brothers took turns flying the craft four more times.

The Wright Brothers

Solution on page 117

Alan Turing

Turing was awarded the Order of the British Empire for his service to his country after World War II. He was awarded this medal for his work on breaking the Engima code and helping the Allies win and end the war. The British royal family presents the award.

START

FINISH

Solution on page 117

Charles Darwin traveled the world on the ship the HMS Beagle. He used his geology tools and took samples of rocks and soils back to the boat to study. He observed many different animal species during his travels, including turtles, finches, and bats. From his observations, he discovered that animals had changed or adapted to better survive in their habitat.

Solution on page 117

George Washington Carver

Carver is best known for his work in agriculture and crop rotation. He taught how farmers could grow different crops, improve the soil and make money too. Planting peanuts and sweet potatoes was good for soil after so many years of growing cotton. Carver traveled the South in his Jesup wagon. It was a mobile classroom used to teach farmers about alternative crops.

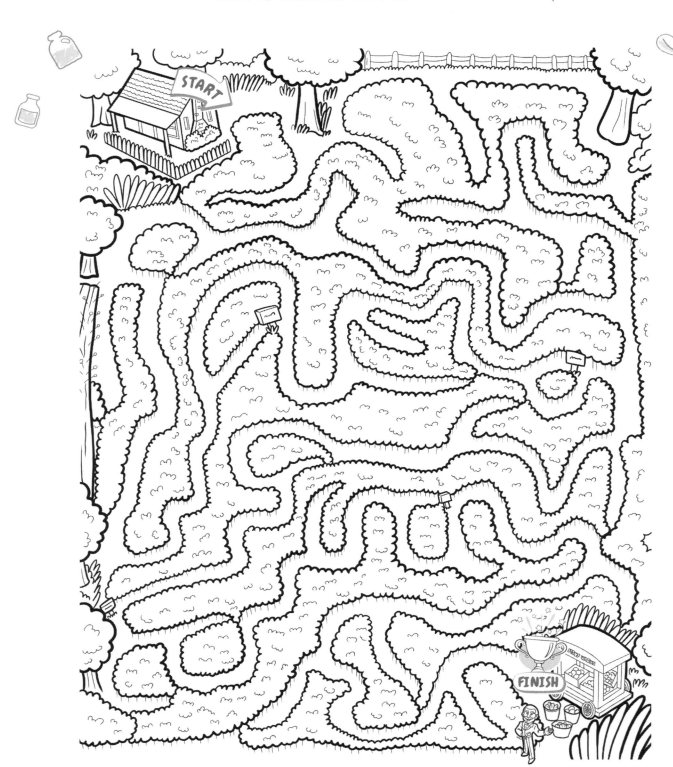

Solution on page 117

The Analytical Machine was created to make calculations. Ada Lovelace created codes in an algorithm. She explained that numbers could be used instead of letters. Ada also theorized a method for the analytical engine to repeat a set of instructions- much the way modern computers do. She believed that one day computers could do art, music, and more. She was right!

Solution on page 117

Women used a "hot comb" that straightened hair. Madam CJ Walker developed a comb that worked better and added it to her hair care line. Cosmetics were created and developed as well.

Solution on page 117

Wolfgang Amadeus (nicknamed Wolfi or Wolfer) was born in 1756 in Salzburg, Austria. A music prodigy, he began playing music on a keyboard at age 4. His sister was also talented, and Mozart's father scheduled performances for the two children all around Europe. The two even performed for royalty.

Solution on page 117

Isaac Newton

After his father died, young Isaac Newton grew up with his grandparents. He was mostly alone and as a result, preferred working on his own as an adult. During his early years, Isaac did not do well in school, and his mother kept him home. His family wanted him to be a farmer, but Issac wanted to be a scientist! At age 18, in the year 1661, he went to Cambridge University.

Solution on page 117

Jane Austen, an author, born in England in 1775, was a literary genius. As a child, Jane and her family would write stories and plays. The family members would act out the roles and wear costumes too. Jane's father encouraged her writing and bought her fine paper to write her stories. At this time, paper was very expensive. This was a special gift.

Frida Kahlo

Kahlo was a Mexican painter. She was famous for her self-portraits and very personal art, as well as her work that was surreal in style. She loved bright colors. When younger, she didn't think of being a painter. Frida loved math and science and wanted to be a doctor.

Solution on page 118

Telescopes were not very powerful in Galileo's day. So he made one better. With his improved telescope, he was able to see the rings of Saturn and the inner moons of Jupiter. Galileo proved that the sun was the center of the universe. The Roman Catholic Church did not want this discovery talked about, but Galileo taught about his discovery and was arrested.

Solution on page 118

Born in London in 1912, Alan attended private school as a child and went on to earn a Ph.D. in mathematics. Shortly after his graduation, World War II began, and Alan Turing played an essential role in helping the Allies win the war.

Solution on page 118

When the Wright Brothers completed their high school years, they opened a bike shop in 1892. They sold and repaired bikes but also made custom bikes for their customers. Seven years later they began to study and experiment with flying.

Solution on page 118

Madam CJ Walker

Sarah Breedlove, who later changed her name to Madam CJ Walker, was the daughter of a slave in Louisiana. She started working at age 10 picking cotton. Years later, she worked as a laundry washerwoman for 1.50 US dollars per day. Sarah Breedlove had great plans and worked hard. She developed hair and cosmetic products for Black women and became America's first self-made millionaire.

Solution on page 118

Some little known facts about Leonardo, are that he was a gifted musician and he slept very little. He played the harpsichord and was known to play the flute. He performed at the homes of the nobility and for his patrons. It has been reported that he only slept 20 minutes every 4 hours when he was working. He even invented a water alarm clock. For this clock, water would drip into a vessel. When the vessel was full it would turnover and trigger rope attached to a pulley. The rope would pull Leonardo's legs up in the air, thus waking him up.

Leonardo da Vinci

Solution on page 118

FINISH

START

George Washington Carver

George Washington Carver was a farmer and agriculturalist. He was an inventor too. He found ways to use sweet potatoes and peanuts for many inventions and products, including rubber, shoe polish, and fabric dye.

Solution on page 118

Beethoven moved to Vienna at the age of 21. Here it is said that he kept a messy house and often leftover food was left lying around. He began to study composition with the famous Joseph Hadyn.

Jane Austen

Jane's novels were witty and humorous; the characters were authentic. The story's plots revolved around romance and finding a husband. However, Jane thought that women could be independent and could have an income of their own. She also believed that women shouldn't worry so much about their appearance.

Solution on page 118

Sir Isaac Newton's family was not wealthy, so to pay for his education, he worked as a valet. A valet is someone who looked after men's clothes. He attended school until 1665, but then the great Plague forced the university to close. He returned home and continued his studies there. He became a physicist, astronomer, and one of the greatest mathematicians of all time.

Solution on page 118

FINISH

START

When Frida Kahlo was 6 years old, she had polio which left her disabled. At age 18 she was in an accident. The injuries left her with severe pain that she dealt with her entire life. Because of the pain, she could no longer continue her studies at medical school. She decided to paint.

START

FINISH

Solution on page 118

Although many inventors were working on the telephone, Bell filed his patent first. Bell started the first telephone company, AT&T, in 1877. AT&T is the largest phone company and mobile communications company in the world. It is valued at over 108 billion US dollars.

Alexander Graham Bell

Solution on page 119

FINISH

START

Albert Einstein

Albert Einstein was born in Germany in 1879. He was a very quiet child and did not speak until he was three years old. When he was five years old, his father gave him a compass. The compass ignited a curiosity in him and sparked his interest in science.

START

FINISH

Solution on page 119

Helen Keller lost her sight and hearing after an illness--possibly scarlet fever--when she was 19 months old. Helen was an angry and unruly toddler, and her parents reached out for someone to help them with their daughter, who could not see or hear. Alexander Graham Bell told them to visit the Perkins School for the Blind. There they met Anne Sullivan. Anne became Helen's teacher.

Solution on page 119

START

FINISH

Leonardo da Vinci

Leonardo da Vinci is considered one of the greatest minds of all time. Leonardo was a painter, a scientist, and an inventor. He was a "Renaissance man" because he was skilled and knowledgeable about so many different subjects.

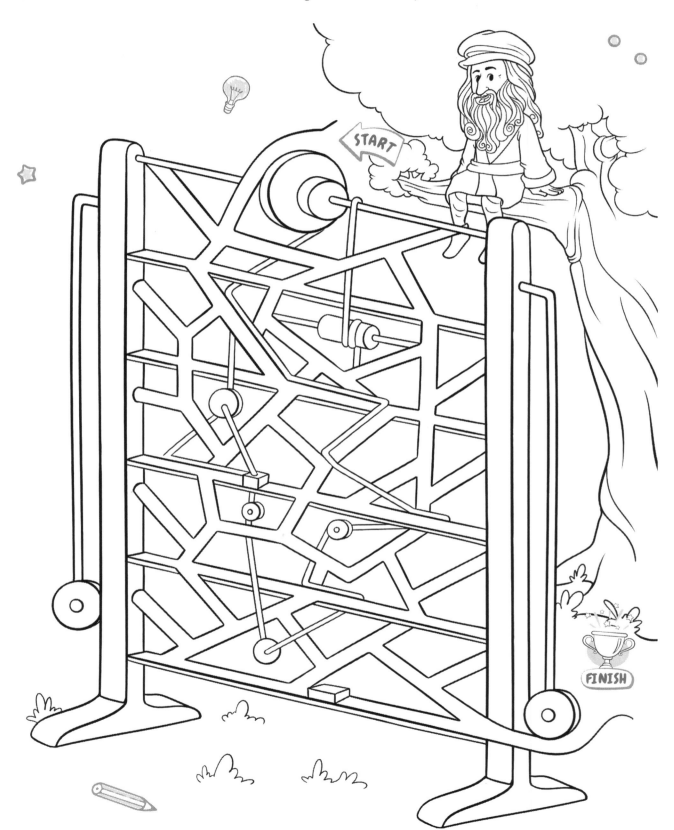

Solution on page 119

Mozart became so famous that throughout the years, many things have been named after him. In Haiti, there is a frog that can produce many different kinds of sounds similar to music notes. The frog is named Eleutherodactylus Amadeus. Around the world there are cafes, cakes and even asteroids with his name.

Solution on page 119

Darwin's travels and studies led to his famous book: *The Origin of Species*. The book details his theory of evolution through natural selection. These theories challenged many accepted ideas on animals and human origins.

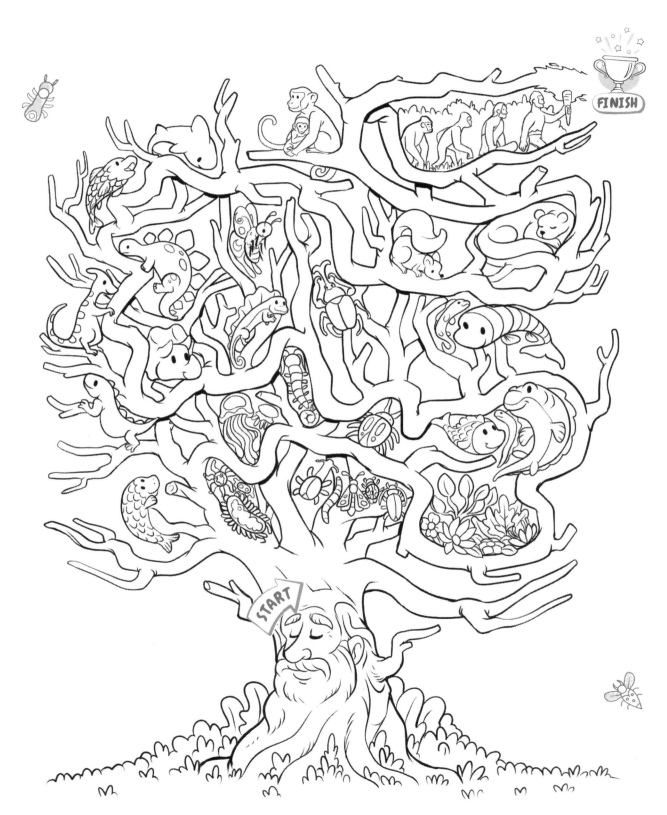

FINISH

START

Solution on page 119

Alan Turing began work on what is now considered "modern" digital programming. This universal machine could decode and follow instructions. He theorized about artificial intelligence. Could a machine think like a human? Turing developed the "Turing Test" to see if machines could think like people.

Solution on page 119

START

FINISH

Wolfgang Amadeus Mozart

Mozart wrote and composed many concertos and symphonies. Mozart learned to play music on the piano, but he could play the violin and other instruments. He was a musical genius. His works included *The Marriage of Figaro*, *Don Giovanni*, and *The Magic Flute*. His last work, called *Requiem*, was not finished before he died.

Solution on page 119

Thomas Edison set up a lab in the US state of New Jersey. Here, he worked on many great inventions that changed history. The phonograph, the light bulb, a movie camera, and an electric pen were all created by Edison. Edison had a never-quit attitude--he tried over 1000 times to perfect the lightbulb! This attitude led to 1093 patents and some life-changing inventions.

Solution on page 119

Rosalind Franklin

Rosalind studied coal in college. This research led to improvements to gas mask filters. The changes to the filters helped and saved soldiers during World War II. She used special cameras and x-rays in her coal research that helped her take the first pictures of DNA strands.

Solution on page 119

From 1861 to 1865, the American Civil War stopped steamboat travel and commerce. Mark Twain, known as Samuel Clemens, could no longer captain riverboats. He became a miner for a short time. He didn't like this job and then began to write. Samuel Clemens adopted the pen name of 'Mark Twain,' a term for '12 feet of water' in steamboat slang.

Solution on page 119

Da Vinci is well known for creating the most famous painting of all time--the Mona Lisa. This painting is valued at 650 million US dollars. Other well-known art masterpieces include *The Last Supper*, *Vitruvian Man*, *Self Portrait*, and *Head of a Woman*.

Solution on page 119

Marco Polo also brought back from China new technology. The compass was first designed by the Chinese. With a compass, land and sea could be explored more easily. In addition, a compass helped make more accurate maps. Marco brought back paper and paper currency. The idea of using paper to buy something of value was new to Europeans.

Solution on page 120

Jane Austen

Jane completed the first draft of a novel when she was just 21 years old. Her brother and father helped get the novels published as women could not participate in business affairs. Her famous books include *Sense and Sensibility*, *Pride and Prejudice*, and *Emma*.

Solution on page 120

As a child, Ford liked to build and fix things. At age 13, his father gave him a pocket watch. He took it apart and reassembled it. Neighbors then gave him their watches any time they didn't work so he could fix them. At age 16, he became an apprentice to a ship builder. He learned to fix and operate steam engines.

Solution on page 120

START

FINISH

Isaac Newton

Cambridge University was closed in 1665 because of the dangerous bubonic plague. Isaac Newton went home. During this time, he constructed sun-dials and windmills. And, his important work on the Laws of Nature began. His theory of gravity formed when sitting in his garden; an apple fell from a tree. He wondered why it fell down and not sideways.

Solution on page 120

Helen Keller could not see or hear. Her teacher, Anne, tried to teach her the word "doll" with sign language felt by her hands. But she didn't understand. Then she tried "mug" and Helen threw the mug across the room. But Helen did finally understand when she put one of Helen's hands under water and spelled the word W --A--T--E--R into her hand.

Solution on page 120

START

FINISH

Galileo Galilei

Galileo loved to study and question. He began to form ideas to test and check. He developed a method to observe and test hypotheses. Galileo invented the Scientific Method that scientists use even today.

Solution on page 120

Alexander Graham Bell may be recognized for his work on telephones, but he also built a hydrofoil. A hydrofoil was a sort of water-skimming boat that operates in a similar way to a plane and set many world records with it!

Solution on page 120

At age 13, Ada designed a flying machine in the shape of a horse and powered by a steam engine. At the age of 17, she was introduced to Charles Babbage. Babbage created and invented an analytical engine that could make advanced calculations. Ada studied the machine and made her notes with algorithms.

Solution on page 120

Edison worked at different jobs as a boy and young man. He sold candy and newspapers on trains. One day, Thomas Edison saved a child from a runaway train car while selling papers. This event led to an opportunity to become a telegraph operator. The child's father gave him the job because he wanted to reward him for being a hero and saving his son.

Solution on page 120

Rosalind Franklin, developed a special "micro camera" to make the famous photo. Scientists around the world saw for the first time that DNA was shaped in a double helix structure. The discovery of the DNA structure led to the rise of virology-the study of viruses.

Solution on page 120

Rachel Carson's first book is called *Under the Sea-Wind*. It tells the story of an eel, a sea bird, and a fish. In the book, the bird is named Silverbar. The fish is called Scomber and the eel is named Anguilla. The book celebrates sea life and animal life around the oceans and shores.

Solution on page 120

FINISH

START

Michelangelo

Some might consider him one of the greatest painters of all time, with his painting of the ceiling of the Sistine Chapel. Michelangelo worked tirelessly on the ceiling. Often he painted for many hours lying on his back. He reported many health issues and body aches from working on the painting. The part of the ceiling where God is touching man, is most famous.

Solution on page 120

Marie Curie worked hard and graduated high school early when she was 15 years old. She spent one year in the country to rest. Marie began work as a governess, and then she started her university studies.

Solution on page 121

Leonardo da Vinci

Throughout his life, Leonardo filled 50 notebooks with sketches, notes, and ideas. These notebooks included pictures of human anatomy, drawings of nature, and diagrams for many inventions. Leonardo designed and built the aerial screw (an early helicopter), a glider in the shape of a bat, a water alarm clock, and a robot.

Solution on page 121

Henry Ford invented a process to make products very quickly called an assembly line. An assembly line is a way of making a product where the job is broken down into many small jobs completed in order. Each worker performs one task, and then the product moves to the next worker who does the next task. Ford's assembly line made the production of cars and other products very quick! Henry Ford also paid his workers excellent wages.

Solution on page 121

Helen Keller

Helen Keller's teacher was Anne Sullivan. She graduated from the Perkins School of the Blind. Anne used sign language when Helen was seven years old. (which Helen felt with her hands) to begin communications. Later, when Helen was 9, Anne taught her to read Braille and to read lips by placing her hand gently on someone's mouth when they spoke. Anne stayed with Helen for 50 years.

Solution on page 121

George loved to learn. He liked studying and reading about plants and animals. There were no schools for Black children in his state, so he traveled to the Midwest to attend school. He studied botany, got his Master's degree, and became the first Black professor of the college.

START

FINISH

Frida Kahlo

Frida Kahlo painted many pictures of herself and exaggerated facial hair, especially her eyebrows in many pictures. 55 of her 143 pictures were self-portraits. She wore brightly colored clothes and many of her self-portraits pictured her with flowers in her hair and butterflies all around.

START

Solution on page 121

FINISH

Albert Einstein learned to play the violin when he was five, and a love for music lasted all his life. He once said if he hadn't become a scientist, he would have become a musician. He went on to study math and physics in school and received his doctorate in math in 1905.

Solution on page 121

During World War II, the Germans used a code-making machine called Enigma to send messages that could not be deciphered. Alan Turing and others worked day and night to devise a way to crack the Enigma code. Turing helped create a machine that could decipher Enigmas messages. It was called Bombe.

Solution on page 121

Henry Ford was an American businessman and entrepreneur. He is best known for his design and manufacture of the Model T car in 1908. The car was affordable and many people in this time period could afford one. The car sold for $850 at first but then the price dropped to $300 when Ford plant got the assembly lines going.

Solution on page 121

Galileo Galilei

Galileo was born during the Renaissance in Pisa, Italy. As a child, Galileo was an excellent student and a musician. He attended school at a monastery and thought of becoming a priest. His father wanted him to be a doctor. While attending medical school, he excelled in mathematics. Galileo almost became a doctor but decided to study math instead.

Solution on page 121

Many have called Ada Lovelace the first computer programmer. Ada knew that machines could do more than just solve math problems. She wrote an algorithm, like a set of instructions, that was similar to computer programs today. She was a forward thinker and a mathematical genius.

Solution on page 121

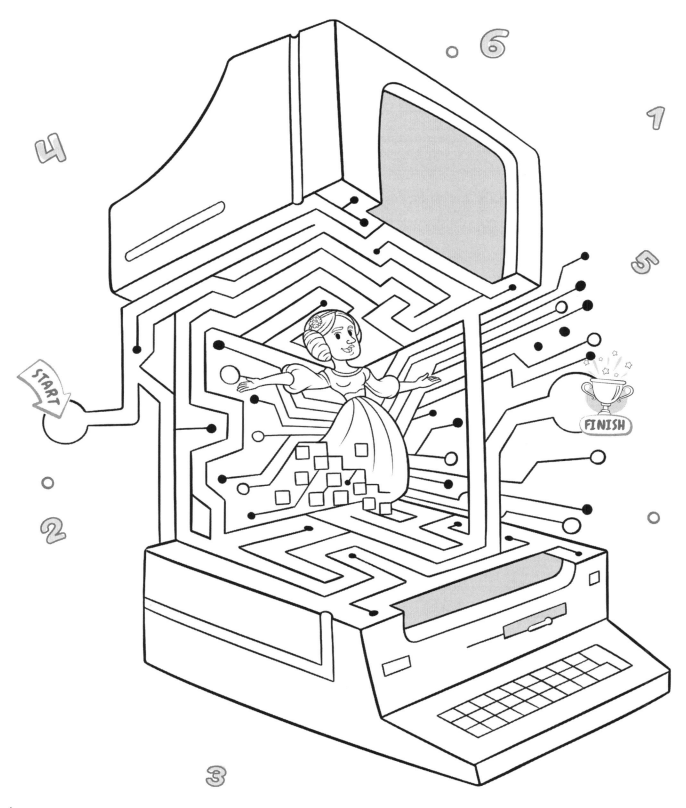

Nikola Tesla

Nikola Tesla worked with Thomas Edison for a time but then built his lab. He didn't have investors to fund his work, so he dug ditches for $2 US dollars per day. Luckily, the A.C induction motor's invention was successful, and he no longer had to dig ditches.

Solution on page 121

Michelangelo considered himself a sculptor. He studied the human body by dissecting cadavers and then made a sculpture of Hercules. He went on and sculpted many other great works. His statue David is considered to be his most famous. But he also sculpted Moses and many others.

Solution on page 122

★★★

Einstein's theories on light and electrons-the photoelectric effect-won him a Nobel Prize in 1921. But he is most famous for his equation E=mc². This theory explained that energy (E) happens when we move masses (m) faster than the speed of light (c²). This equation helped change physics as we know it.

Solution on page 122

After Mark Twain's father died when he was 11, he left school, took a typesetter job, and became a printer's apprentice. Young Samuel (Mark Twain's actual name) visited libraries and read books constantly to educate himself. His dream was to become a steamboat pilot, and he trained and got his license in 1858.

Solution on page 122

Ada Lovelace

Ada Lovelace was the daughter of the famous poet Lord Byron. Her mother began young Ada's special education at age 4. As a girl, her classes would have centered around needlework, learning a foreign language, music, and how to manage a household. However, her mother loved math. Her nickname was the Princess of Parallelograms. She ensured her daughter learned math and science.

Solution on page 122

The Wright Brothers published and sold a weekly newspaper. The newspaper was called the West Side News. They also published a bicycle parts catalog, materials for a church, and a school newspaper.

Solution on page 122

Thomas is considered the greatest inventor of all time. Later in life, he worked on creating batteries and worked on supplying electricity to homes using electrical lines. Edison's inventions changed the world and impacted every citizen.

Solution on page 122

Rosalind Franklin was a serious and dedicated scientist, But she also had hobbies. She loved the country of France and liked to go back-packing in the French Alps.

Solution on page 122

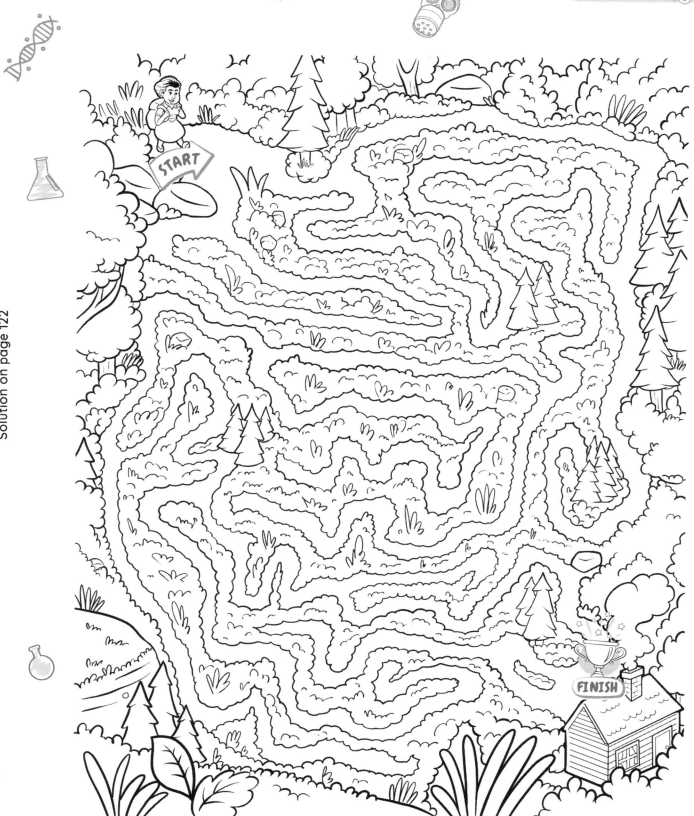

Marie Curie

After finishing high school, Marie Curie wanted to continue learning. But, women were not allowed to go to college in Poland. So, for six years after high school, she worked to pay for her sister's education in France. But she studied on her own! She also attended Warsaw's "Flying University" This was a network of classes held in secret. Often the classes were held in people's homes. The locations of the classes frequently changed so that the Russian authorities would not find them and arrest the students and teachers.

START

FINISH

Solution on page 122

⭐⭐⭐

At age 17, Nikola Tesla suffered from a sickness called cholera. His father told him he wanted him to become a priest, but he could become an engineer if he survived the illness. And he did! He soon became a student at the Austrian Polytechnic School. However, he never graduated. In 1884 he left his home to go to the United States, where he became a naturalized citizen.

Nikola Tesla

Solution on page 122

Ludwig van Beethoven

Ludwig began to lose his hearing in his late 20's, but this did not stop him from composing. At first, when his hearing was only mildly impaired, he would use ear trumpets to help him compose at the piano. He would also use a wooden stick between his teeth to feel the vibrations when he played.

Solution on page 122

Rachel Carson was a leader in the conservation movement and wrote about eco-systems, how islands are formed, erosion, and climate change. She warned about the dangers of chemical pesticides. Her books started a movement that led to the creation of the Environmental Protection Agency.

Solution on page 122

George Washington Carver

George Washington Carver was raised by the owners of the farm, in which his mother had worked and been a slave. He was encouraged to go to school and was a bright student. However, he did not work in the fields with his brother because he was a sickly child. He worked in the home, did laundry, cooked, and worked the kitchen gardens where he grew to love plants. He used these skills to earn money as he grew older. He also learned to play the piano.

Solution on page 122

Frida Kahlo's work had much symbolism. Butterflies represented her rebirth after her accident. Hummingbirds symbolized hope and good luck. Some of her paintings had medical imagery because she spent so much time in hospitals throughout her life after her accident.

Solution on page 123

Alexander Graham Bell

Alexander Graham Bell invented a metal detector and a graphophone that recorded and played sounds. He considered his most significant invention to be the photophone. This device could turn sound and images into light and send them long distances. Alexander Graham Bell's fascination with the science of sounds led to many great inventions!

Solution on page 123

Sarah Breedlove changed her name to Madam CJ Walker after her husband. With her daughter's help managing the business Madam CJ's success grew. She trained other Black women to sell products and start their businesses. She was an activist and lobbied in Washington DC, and was a donor to charities. Madam CJ drove electric cars and loved to go to the cinema to see movies.

Solution on page 123

Isaac Newton

Isaac Newton wrote *Principia*, which explained the principles of gravity, motion, and lots of math. He "invented" calculus and studied optics with the use of prisms. Albert Einstein once said that Isaac Newton might have been the smartest person of all time.

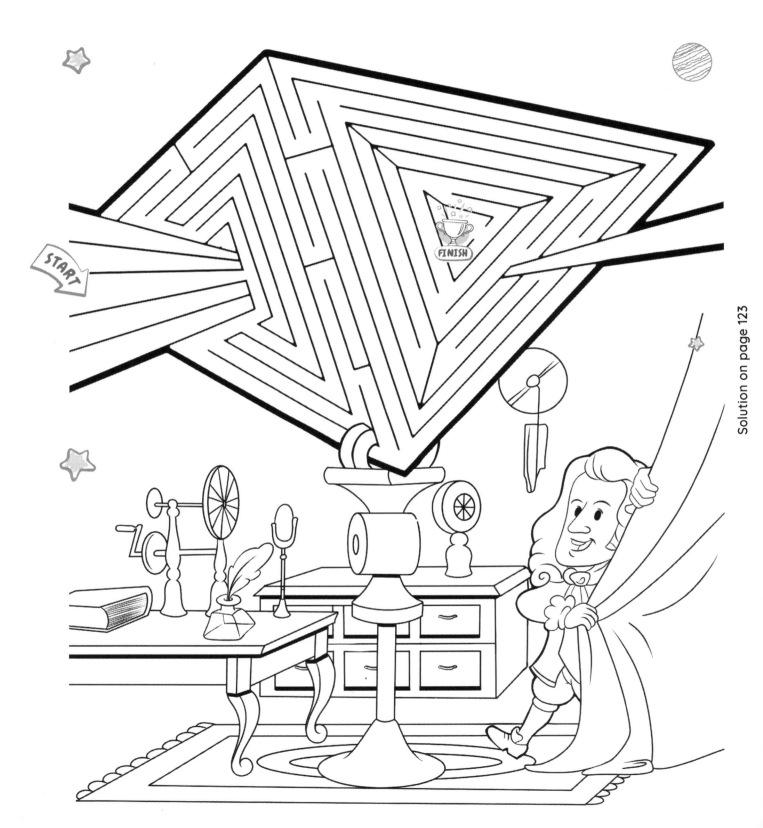

Solution on page 123

With her husband Pierre, Marie discovered two elements: Radium and Polonium. Her discoveries led to advancements in the area of X-rays and a theory of radioactivity. She was the first woman to win the Nobel prize in physics and the first person to win a second Nobel in the field of chemistry.

Solution on page 123

Henry Ford and Thomas Edison (inventor of the light bulb) were best friends. Henry even worked with Edison at the Edison Illuminating Company. It was his job to keep the lights on in the city of Detroit. While working together, Henry showed Edison his plans for an automobile.

Solution on page 123

In Jane Austen's life, women who possessed wealth often wore fancy and beautiful hats to shade their faces from the sun. Families with wealth and high social standing also owned beautiful carriages and horses.

Solution on page 123

Galileo spent the last eight years of his life under house arrest. Galileo's work with the telescope, as well as experiments and discoveries with pendulums, velocity, and ramps, helped thinkers of the past and today better understand the world and universe.

Solution on page 123

Helen Keller learned to read using Braille and to write using a Braille typewriter. She even learned to speak. Helen was the first blind/deaf person to earn a college degree. She wrote 12 books and was an advocate for the disabled. She had a connection to music (she could feel the beats) and animals (that she loved to touch.) Her favorite animal was a dog.

Solution on page 123

START

FINISH

Nikola Tesla

Nikola Tesla invented many things that changed people's everyday lives. He filed patents for generators, wireless lighting, radio communications, x-ray imaging, and more. He created a remote control boat which many feel launched the field of modern-day robotics.

Solution on page 123

Rachel Carson wrote her most famous book *Silent Spring* after a friend wrote and told her about bird life being harmed by pesticides. For her work, she was awarded the Presidential Medal of Freedom many years after her death.

Solution on page 123

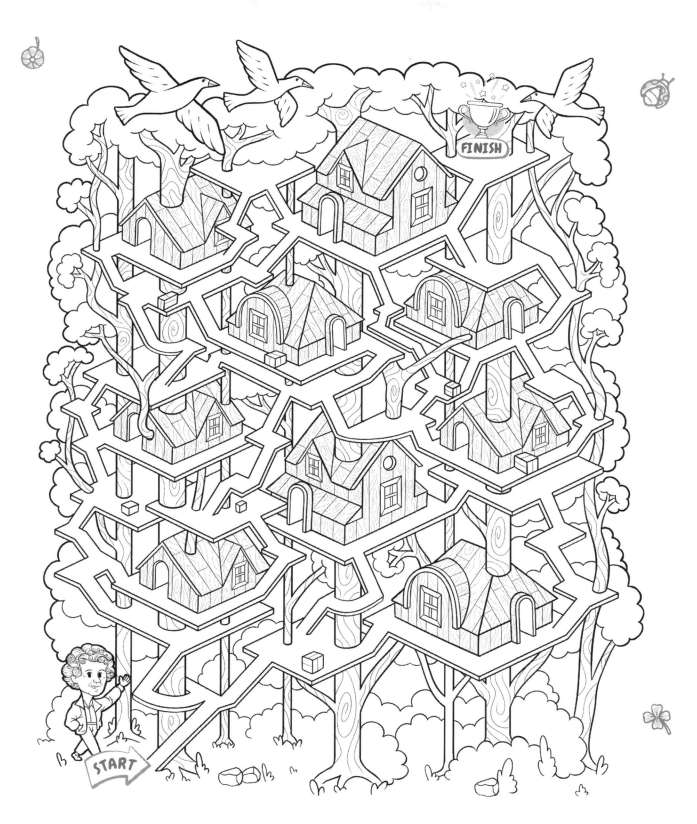

Ludwig van Beethoven was completely deaf by age 45. But he still wrote music! He had perfect pitch when he was younger, and he could remember each sound and note in his mind.

Solution on page 123

★★★

In 1546, Michelangelo was over 70 years old, but he was given one the most important jobs of his life. St Peter's Basilica had been damaged and partially demolished. Many architects had been working on drawings to rebuild the building. Michelangelo made better plans for a larger and stronger dome. St Peter's Basilica still stands today and is one of the greatest monuments to Christianity.

Solution on page 124

★★★

Mark Twain

Mark Twain's first success as a writer came in 1865 when his funny story *'The Celebrated Jumping Frog of Calaveras County'* was published in a New York weekly, *'The Saturday Press.'* The story started his writing career.

Solution on page 124

Marco Polo encountered many unfamiliar animals on his journeys. He documented his encounters with elephants, monkeys and crocodiles and even rode camels across Arabia. Once when he first saw a rhinoceros, he thought he was seeing a mythical unicorn.

Solution on page 124

FINISH

START

Throughout his life, Albert Einstein worked on his "theory of everything." He believed that all science fields could be connected and all the forces of the universe could be explained. This theory, however, was never proven.

Solution on page 124

This is what you'll need

pencil

crayons or markers

scissors

glue

1 Building the maze.

a Cut out the 2 pieces (pp.115 and 117).

b Glue them together.

2 Solve the maze. Use a pencil, then use a different color for each correct path through the maze.

3 Color the pictures if desired.

13: **The Wright Brothers**

14: **Alexander Graham Bell**

15: **Wolfgang Amadeus Mozart**

16: **Madam C. J. Walker**

17: **Nikola Tesla**

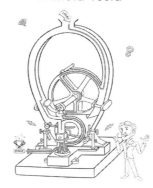

18: **Rosalind Franklin**

19: **Thomas Edison**

20: **Marco Polo**

21: **Michelangelo**

22: **Charles Darwin**

23: **Marie Curie**

24: **Ludwig van Beethoven**

Solutions

25: Mark Twain

26: Marco Polo

27: Rachel Carson

28: Charles Darwin

29: The Wright Brothers

30: Alan Turing

31: Charles Darwin

32: George Washington Carver

33: Ada Lovelace

34: Madam C. J. Walker

35: Wolfgang Amadeus Mozart

36: Isaac Newton

37: Jane Austen

38: Frida Kahlo

39: Galileo Galilei

40: Alan Turing

41: The Wright Brothers

42: Madam C.J. Walker

43: Leonardo da Vinci

44: George Washington Carver

45: Ludwig van Beethoven

46: Jane Austen

47: Isaac Newton

48: Frida Kahlo

49: Alexander Graham Bell

50: Albert Einstein

51: Helen Keller

52 Leonardo Di Vinci

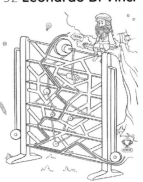

53: Wolfgang Amadeus Mozart

54: Charles Darwin

55: Alan Turing

56: Wolfgang Amadeus Mozart

57: Thomas Edison

58: Rosalind Franklin

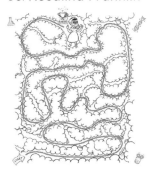

59: Mark Twain

60: Leonardo da Vinci

61: Marco Polo

62: Jane Austen

63: Henry Ford

64: Isaac Newton

65: Helen Keller

66: Galileo Galilei

67: Alexander Graham Bell

68: Ada Lovelace

69: Thomas Edison

70: Rosalind Franklín

71: Rachel Carson

72: Michelangelo

73: Marie Curie

74: Leonardo da Vinci

75: Henry Ford

76: Helen Keller

77: George Washington Carver

78: Frida Kahlo

79: Albert Einstein

80: Alan Turing

81: Henry Ford

82: Galileo Galilei

83: Ada Lovelace

84: Nikola Tesla

85: **Michelangelo**

86: **Albert Einstein**

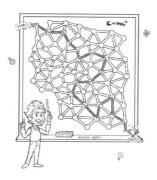

87: **Mark Twain**

88: **Ada Lovelace**

89: **The Wright Brothers**

90: **Thomas Edison**

91: **Rosalind Franklin**

92: **Marie Curie**

93: **Nikola Tesla**

94: **Ludwig van Beethoven**

95: **Rachel Carson**

96: **George Washington Carver**

97: Frida Kahlo

98: Alexander Graham Bell

99: Madam C.J. Walker

100: Isaac Newton

101: Marie Curie

102: Henry Ford

103: Jane Austen

104: Galileo Galilei

105: Helen Keller

106: Nikola Tesla

107: Rachel Carson

108: Ludwig van Beethoven

⭐ ⭐ ⭐

109: Michelangelo

110: Mark Twain

111 Marco Polo

112: Albert Einstein

MegaMaze

Finished the book?
Well done!

Send us a video and receive a
certificate diploma from Megageex!
support@megageex.com

How can you get more
out of MegaGeex?

Subscribe to our newsletter at
www.MegaGeex.com and follow us on
Instagram and Facebook
to receive free activity pages to inspire
your kids.

 www.MegaGeex.com

 MegaGeex

MegaGeexCom

Printed in Great Britain
by Amazon